THE UNIQUE
ONE MINUTE SALES METHODS
THAT REALLY WORK!

P9-DNO-663

"I am recommending THE ONE MINUTE SALES PERSON to all our sales people, because it will surely increase the sales of anyone who applies this approach."
W. T. Lambert, Vice President and Director of Sales
KELLOGG U.S. FOOD PRODUCTS DIVISION

"Follow the wise advice in this great book and become the great sales person of your dreams!"
Og Mandino, author of
THE GREATEST SALESMAN IN THE WORLD

"One easy way to begin to turn the 'close to the customer' concept into practical reality is to read this book."
Robert Waterman, co-author of
IN SEARCH OF EXCELLENCE

"This book provokes...It requires us to think...analyze...be solution-oriented, and, above all, realize that the fuel for motivation comes from within ourselves!"
Shelby H. Carter, Vice President/General Sales Manager
XEROX CORPORATION

THE UNIQUE
ONE MINUTE SALES METHODS
THAT REALLY WORK!

THE UNIQUE
ONE MINUTE SALES METHODS
THAT REALLY WORK!

Avon Books are available at special quantity discounts for bulk purchases for sales promotions, premiums, fund raising or educational use. Special books, or book excerpts, can also be created to fit specific needs.

For details write or telephone the office of the Director of Special Markets, Avon Books, Dept. FP, 1350 Avenue of the Americas, New York, New York 10019, 1-800-238-0658.

The One Minute $ales Person™

Spencer Johnson, M.D.

The One Minute $ales Person

Co-authored with Larry Wilson

AVON BOOKS ♦ NEW YORK

Dedicated to the memory of
TOM UTNE
who helped to make
the world a better place.

AVON BOOKS
A division of
The Hearst Corporation
1350 Avenue of the Americas
New York, New York 10019

Copyright © 1984 by Candle Communications Corporation
Published by arrangement with William Morrow and Company, Inc.
Library of Congress Catalog Card Number: 84-61414
ISBN: 0-380-70151-0

First Avon Books Printing: September 1986

AVON TRADEMARK REG. U.S. PAT. OFF. AND IN OTHER COUNTRIES, MARCA REGISTRADA, HECHO EN U.S.A.

Printed in the U.S.A.

RA   20   19

The Symbol

The One Minute Sales Person's symbol—a one-minute readout from the face of a modern digital watch—is intended to remind us to take a minute to look at each customer as a PERSON. And to realize that *they* are our most important resource.

Introduction

The One Minute $ales Person presents you with a "new school" of selling attitudes and skills that you can use more successfully in today's marketplace.

It is based on concisely distilled experience, insight, and advice from some of the nation's most successful sales people—as well as from the vice-presidents of marketing and sales from more than one hundred major corporations in practically every industry.

This book also includes the wisdom gained by The Wilson Learning Corporation of Minneapolis, a company that has, for the past twenty years, trained more than 300,000 sales people, and has, for the last ten years, collected data on how customers like to buy. This current "customer view" is core to the book's perspective.

The One Minute $ales Person follows the success of the international best seller *The One Minute Manager*. We encourage you to read that book as well so you fully benefit from the second part of this book, "Selling Me On Me": a self-management method for sales people.

We hope you will use what you learn from *The One Minute $ales Person*, in addition to what you already know about selling, and that you too will soon make more sales with less stress.

—SPENCER JOHNSON, M.D.
LARRY WILSON

Contents

ONCE there was a very successful sales person.

He felt more than successful. He felt prosperous!

He enjoyed peace of mind, financial independence, security, good health, and an enjoyable social life. He had the respect and admiration of all who knew him.

Many people wanted to do business with him. And even more people wanted him as a friend.

However, he hadn't always been so successful.

He could remember the many years when he tried harder but did no better than most people.

Now he was glad that he knew what he knew. And, more important, that he put it to *use*.

The man smiled as he thought about how easily he had finally learned to prosper.

He realized early in life that almost everyone who succeeded was really an effective sales person, whether he or she realized it or not.

"Successful business people," he observed, "sell others on the value of their services. Successful parents sell their children on leading happy and productive lives. Successful leaders sell their abilities to bring people what they want. Even successful scientists sell their ideas to those who provide the research funds which enable them to do their work."

The man remembered thinking when he was still in college, "Perhaps if I can learn to sell well, then I will do well in whatever I undertake."

And so the man had tried his hand at different sales jobs while he was still in school.

The few times he succeeded, it was exhilarating. He thought, "It's like they're buying me!" However, when he tried to sell but failed, he felt rejected. He told himself, "I'm just not cut out to sell."

After he graduated with a degree in marketing, he realized he had learned very little about sales.

Marketing, he learned, was about doing research to learn what people wanted, creating the products and services that people wanted, pricing them competitively, and then making it easy for people to buy.

But marketing and sales sometimes seemed at odds.

In his first real sales job for a major firm, he learned about the importance of product knowledge and about how to "pitch it to the prospects"—to get appointments, to answer objections, and to close a sale.

But the more he was involved in sales, the more he got the impression that the underlying presumption was that the customer did not want to buy the product.

It was as though a sales person's job was to be smart enough and tough enough to get people to do what they didn't really want to do—to buy. And the best salesmen, it seemed, found a way to do it.

It didn't make sense to him.

For a while he enjoyed the challenge. The tougher it got, the more he called on his self-discipline and persistence. He forced himself, for instance, to go out and make one more call each day than he really wanted to. It added up: He made over two hundred more sales calls each year. And it had paid off. He made more sales than most. And more money.

So he decided to add another one hundred calls a year. But a strange thing occurred. His sales did not increase much. And he wasn't having fun. He pushed himself even harder. And then he began to feel the stress.

It came from many sources. He had to close so many sales each month—his quota. And it was easy to measure his performance. At times, he wished that he had a job like other folks where it wasn't so easy to tell how well or how poorly he was doing.

Often he wasn't treated well by the people he called on. Many acted as if he were out to get them.

He felt there was too much to do and too little time to do it in. Sometimes he felt unprepared.

He had great expectations for his increasing income, but he had doubts sometimes about making it.

Ironically, he knew that if his sales manager didn't put the pressure on him, he would put it on himself.

Selling was going to become more enjoyable soon, but the man did not know it yet.

Like other sales people, the man often felt the quiet fear of rejection. Some people would inevitably turn him down. He did not look forward to such times.

To make matters worse, as much as he wanted to deny it, he saw how increasingly complicated the selling process seemed to be in today's changing world. He had been repeating the same words that had given him his sales for years. Why weren't they working now?

Then he remembered an unusual story.

From time to time, he had heard the name of a legendary salesman—one who made more sales than anyone else and yet apparently had more leisure time than most people to enjoy his extraordinary success.

Someone said he was called The One Minute Salesman—although the man did not know why.

The man thought there must be a better way—a way to restore the sense of fun and success in selling he occasionally had.

So he decided to be bold enough to find out for himself. He decided to ask.

T HE voice at the other end of the telephone took him by surprise. The wealthy and respected "salesman" he'd expected turned out to be the chairman of the board of a major corporation.

"I would be very happy to meet with you," said the CEO, "and from the tone of your voice I think I know just what you'd like to talk about."

The caller felt a little naked. "Do I sound that desperate?"

"No," replied the CEO. "You sound like a man who has taken the traditional approach to selling about as far as it can go."

"I'm not the first, I take it?"

"That's right. And, like others before you, you sound like you're open and ready to learn. That's why I've agreed to meet with you. Drop by anytime tomorrow." And with that, the CEO hung up.

The man began to look forward to the next day's meeting.

Soon after the man entered the elegant offices, he expressed surprise at meeting a chief executive officer with such a strong sales background.

His host pointed out that, in fact, many of the *Fortune* 1000 CEOs come from the marketing and sales departments. He explained that he had sold products and services for many years. He now sat on the boards of many other companies because he knew how to sell people on important ideas, too.

Looking around the office, the visitor noticed a small plaque on one of the lamp tables. It read: *Production minus sales equals scrap*.

The executive noted, "Even valuable ideas can wind up on the scrap pile just because they weren't sold.

"For example, I am now serving on a panel of community leaders who are concerned with both keeping our nation strong and avoiding the destruction of an all-out war. As good as some of the ideas to solve this problem might be, how much good would they do if either side decided not to buy the answers?"

"Not much. I can see you're still a salesman."

"I think *every* successful person is—in the best sense of that word," replied the prosperous executive.

The man began slowly to reveal his own problem. "I used to think I knew what selling was all about, but now I'm not so sure. It seems like I'm doing everything right . . . but . . ."

"You mean," the older man interjected, "you've read all the books, you go to motivational rallies every chance you get, and you work many nights and weekends?"

"How did you know?"

"And now you've reached the point of diminishing returns, working longer hours while your sales figures are standing still. . . ."

"That's right—and I'm enjoying it less."

"Well, I don't mean to rub it in," the older man said, "but you might be interested to know that my record sales years were accomplished in twenty-hour weeks."

"Ouch," replied the visitor, "but that's what I need to hear. I've heard you're pretty good. They call you The One Minute Salesman. Why *is* that?"

His host shot back, "I'm called that only by those people who do not understand my success."

The man wondered what was wrong.

The chief executive smiled. He wrote something on a piece of paper and handed it to the visitor. It read: *The One Minute $ales Person*.

"Why Sales *Person* instead of Sales*man*?"

"I once had a great manager," said the CEO, "a man we called The One Minute Manager because he got such great results in so little time—in just a few key minutes.

"He taught me a simple principle and then encouraged me to adapt it in my own way, and apply it to sales.

"Now thinking of myself as a One Minute Sales *Person* helps me remember the most important secret in selling. It is as simple as this:

*

Behind every sale

is a PERSON.

*

"The other person—the one so many people call a customer or prospect—is, in fact, a *person*. If you treat him or her as a *commodity*, or as anything but a person, you reduce yourself to a *peddler*."

"Then why did you write out $ALES PERSON with a dollar sign?"

"I do that because frankly it reminds me of one of my personal goals: to make money."

The visitor liked that answer, but wasn't sure how it fit. The CEO explained.

"Part of your problem is that you think there is a contradiction. The fact is, if I'm consistently making money, it is almost always a sure sign I am adding value to the other *person*—to the buyer."

The visitor said, "That's sure not part of my thinking when I'm out there scratching to make a buck!"

"That could be why you're scratching so hard."

The CEO's words were penetrating, yet seemed so simple that they didn't fully register. "Tell me about the One Minute part," said the visitor.

"There are several key minutes in each sale. When I say that behind every sale there is a person, I really mean it in two ways: One person is the buyer; the other person is the seller.

"The key minutes in One Minute Selling are those that apply to each—the buyer and the seller.

"And so there are two parts to One Minute Selling: Selling to others and Selling to Me.

The older man asked, "Do you know the 'eighty/twenty' rule?"

"Sure." The visitor felt on more solid ground now. "Eighty percent of our results are produced by about twenty percent of what we do. And eighty percent of our sales are accounted for by twenty percent of the customers. . . ."

The other man added, "And twenty percent of the people on most sales forces make almost eighty percent of the total sales."

"Yes," sighed the visitor. "It seems I'm always trying to get into or stay in that top twenty percent. But what's that got to do with the One Minute Selling?"

"Long ago I set out to identify and understand what the best twenty percent do differently. As I studied what made up those differences, it became clear that it was only a matter of investing a few minutes to do those few things that separated the best from the average.

"After I got crystal clear what those differences are, and when those minutes occur, my sales results improved dramatically.

"Don't think me inconsiderate but let me ask you very directly, Do you know what the key minutes are in your selling style? Or do you spend time and energy doing the unnecessary? If so, you are an 'unconscious' sales person."

"Unconscious?" the man bristled.

The older man took his visitor off the hook. "I certainly don't know everything about selling. I doubt that anyone does. But I do know what the key minutes are for me. And you deserve to know what yours are. When you do, you will sell more quickly."

The man saw that The One Minute Sales Person was a tough character but he could sense that the older man *cared*. The visitor's defensiveness began to disappear.

"Some of the key minutes are actually very simple," said the CEO, "but learning them now wouldn't be much use. That is, not until you become clear on why I wrote PERSON, and why I wrote $ALES with a dollar sign.

"Making money is important. It is one of my *goals*. But it is not my *purpose* in life—nor even in selling."

"Making money is not your purpose in selling? That's hard to follow. Why else would I be out there?"

"I suggest that when you can answer that question, your whole career will turn around. It is the lesson of The Wonderful Paradox."

The very successful sales person admitted, "I used to view the world as a tough dog-eat-dog environment in which I was afraid I wasn't going to do very well. That is, until I discovered how practical the paradox was—especially when I finally started to *use* it—in sales and in my life. I'm still amazed by its power!"

The visitor wanted to know, "What is this wonderful paradox?"

*

The 'Wonderful Paradox'

*I have more fun and enjoy
more financial success*

*when I stop trying to
get what I want*

*and start helping other people
get what they want.*

*

The man did not understand. "I'd like that. But my company's purpose is for me to make a profit!"

The One Minute Sales Person smiled. "Would you say, 'Sir, you may be wondering about the purpose of my call. It's to make a little profit for my company'?"

"No, I don't think that would go over very well."

"No, of course not. What would you think of a person who sat in front of a cold stove and said, 'As soon as you give me heat, I'll put in some wood'?"

"I would say he didn't quite understand the way things work in the real world."

"You're right," The One Minute Sales Person said. "And the best companies realize this as well. They know they must first fulfill their purpose and then they will make money. And the best sales people do the very same thing. They do first things first."

The man wanted to understand. "What do you *do* to help other people get what *they* want?"

"What *I* do is not as important as what you will decide to do when you are selling.

"What you do to sell successfully will probably be somewhat different from what I and others do. You will develop your own uniquely successful style.

"You will discover what to do for yourself very easily once you understand and decide to start 'Selling On Purpose.'"

The man felt ready for a change. He wanted to find a better way. "What does that mean," he asked, "Selling On Purpose?"

"**P**URPOSE in selling can be thought of on two levels," The One Minute Sales Person said.

"First, Selling On Purpose means that I am usually *conscious* of what I am doing. I am not unconsciously repeating a memorized sales routine. On each sales call I am doing what I am doing consciously—on purpose.

"The second, deeper level of Selling On Purpose is, however, where the real power is.

"Do you appreciate the difference yet between a goal (for example, making money) and a purpose?"

"I'm not sure. I would say a goal is something you accomplish. It has a beginning and an end . . . while a purpose is more ongoing and gives meaning to our lives. I guess when people have a purpose in life, they enjoy everything they do more!"

"A very good start! Now, have you ever had a goal you wanted to reach, accomplished that goal, and then found out that it didn't make you happy?"

"Yes, but I thought it was wrong to feel that way."

"Your feeling is shared by many people. That's because people go on chasing goals to prove something that doesn't have to be proved: that they're already worthwhile. Of course, goals are very important in helping us get what we want. But too often we run around using them to get what we already have—our worth."

The guest winced. "How can I tell the difference between my goals and my purpose?"

"Have you ever taken the Tombstone Test?"

"No, I think I would have remembered that."

"Well, it can help you figure out purpose. Ask yourself, 'What would I like to have written on my tombstone?' That is, 'What was my purpose in life?'

"If what you are doing to make a living doesn't complement your purpose in life, you are going to be unhappy and you will find it harder to succeed.

"Do you want your tombstone to read *He won the sales contest* or *He moved a lot of product?* Or would you like your tombstone to read *He helped many people get what* they *wanted. And so he got what he wanted?*

The man sat thinking. "I never thought of it that way." Then he admitted, "I'm not so sure I know what people really want."

"What do *you* want?" the older man asked. "When you answer that you will probably know what other people want."

"I guess I want to feel good . . . about what I am doing . . . and especially about myself."

"Exactly!" The One Minute Sales Person exclaimed. "Now you are getting very close to the core power of One Minute Selling—to the purpose!

"It is helping people get what you want to get.

"Let me show you something I have written down," The One Minute Sales Person said. "I carry it in my wallet and look at it often. It is my selling *purpose*.

"Whether I am selling a service, a product, or an idea to someone, I always do better when I remember to Sell On Purpose." The card read:

*

MY SELLING PURPOSE

*is to help people get
the good <u>feelings</u> they want*

*about what they bought
and about themselves.*

*

The man nodded his head and smiled. "Other people want the same thing I want," he thought. He had the answer inside him all the time. It amazed him. "We do not just need other people. Or need to help other people. *We are other people!*

"To tell you the truth, it had not occurred to me to have such a purpose. I just had a lot of goals."

"The fastest way to achieve your goals," the successful sales person said, "is to stay on purpose.

"Has it occurred to you that you are already adding value to your customers?

"The fact is, with a product or service you believe in, selling is *inherently* purposeful. You do add value. You help people solve problems, seize opportunities, and, by acting, feel better about themselves. You can either recognize that fact or not."

"What's the difference if you *don't* recognize it?"

"Are you saying you don't *care*?"

"I guess I care. Actually I'm not sure."

"Frankly, that's probably been your biggest problem. You can either be blind to the fact that you are contributing—and go right on trying to get your hands in your customers' pockets—and not feeling all that great about yourself in the process—or you can give yourself credit for the fact that you *are* serving, helping, contributing, making a difference—adding value."

"I guess it comes down to caring about your customers, doesn't it?"

The One Minute Sales Person—the man who had made more sales than practically anyone else and done it in less time—kept silent. He let his visitor hear the echo of his own wisdom.

It comes down to caring about your customers, doesn't it?

"Now you have it. I couldn't tell you the answer myself, because you'd have thought I was preaching. But caring is what purpose is all about."

"I see what you mean. A customer can tell if you care or not. I used to care a lot, when I was just starting out, but I guess I got into a rut. No wonder fewer people bought from me."

"And no wonder selling stopped being fun for you."

"I can see we're not just talking about fulfillment or fun. We're talking about customers who trust me and give me referrals and stick with me for the long haul."

"Now you're getting at my *real* secret. That's how I made so many sales in so little time. My satisfied customers would advise other people to buy from me. Often they'd call me—and I didn't even have to sell!"

"When you put it that way, Selling On Purpose isn't an issue of being *nice,* but of being *smart.*"

"That's why we started with Purpose. It is the single major difference that sets apart the top twenty percent from the other eighty percent."

"Let me ask you this," the visitor said. "When I am out there in the real world, how will I remember to Sell On Purpose?"

"Like all One Minute Selling, it is easy.

"I just invest a minute when I am selling to ask myself: *Am I more concerned with trying to get what I want? Or am I really helping other people get what they want?*"

"So," the man realized, "when I see that I'm thinking about myself I just get right back 'on purpose' and focus on the other guy. That *is* easy."

"But remember," the CEO added, "the slogans and tombstone legends and reminders are just that—reminders. Selling On Purpose is an intention, a way of life, *the philosophy from which you operate*—not a slogan. To put it your way, it's *caring*."

"Caring is a very powerful word for me."

"Then that's exactly what you need to bring back into your sales life. I've seen it over and over: When sales people are aware of their purpose, of what really turns them on, and invest that into everything they do, they not only sell their products and services more easily . . ."

"They have more fun!" The visitor began to feel much of his frustration—the guilt and struggle and need to keep proving himself—fading now. Something more valuable was becoming available to him—a part of himself he had forgotten about. He felt a pride that he hadn't known before.

"What feels better to you?" the man was asked, "trying hard to get what you want—your sales quota, for example"—the man frowned—"or simply helping other people get what they really want?" He smiled.

Knowing the answer, the older man said:

*

I quickly reduce my stress
because I no longer try
to get people to do
what they don't want to do.

When I sell On Purpose,
it's like swimming downstream.

*

"You're like most of us. You feel less stress and you'll sell more when you help the other person.

"It was true for me and it'll be more so for you."

"Why more for me?" the man asked.

"Because today's marketplace depends more than ever on the sales person. Products are becoming more and more alike. As you know, people now go to 'marts'—large convention halls—where they can see all the competing products and services. They can see their alternatives. People are in fact more confused because they have so many choices.

"What do you think will be important to people when they buy from among so many similar products? Imagine yourself as the buyer."

"Well, I'd like to trust the person and the company I buy from and to have good service. Trust and service—that's what I'd buy."

The One Minute Sales Person agreed. "And so will millions of other people. That's why the sales person who Sells On Purpose is going to do very well. Because he or she will provide people with trust and service."

The CEO added, "I can see this very easily in our company. When we change a sales person in a territory where we have the same product or service, the same pricing and the same competition, our sales can rise or fall on the reputation of the sales person.

"Selling On Purpose is the best investment a person can make in present and future sales."

The One Minute Sales Person went to his desk, picked up a list, and said, "This may interest you.

"All of the people on this list—men and women—feel they are more successful since they've learned how to be a One Minute Sales Person. After they learn to Sell On Purpose, they use selling methods—with others and with themselves—that take only a minute or so to do. Some of the methods I taught them; others they developed on their own.

"They have various backgrounds and come from various ethnic groups. Some are young; others are older. Several are professionals who sell very different kinds of products or services. Others are people who are not involved in sales in the usual sense but they successfully sell their ideas to other people and thus have more success in their work.

"Pick any half dozen and talk with them. You'll soon discover that these principles work in varying degrees for almost everybody. They are based on universal principles about the way people think, feel, and act.

"I think you will find that they not only Sell On Purpose but they are also very good at 'the brilliant basic'—that is, those things that obviously help them make a sale but which most people forget to do.

"And after you speak with as many successful people as you like, please feel free to return. I'd be happy to explain *why* One Minute Selling works so well—for the buyer and for the seller."

The One Minute Sales Person rose, shook hands with his visitor, and walked him to the door.

As the man looked at the list of people, he said, "Thank you. I'll begin immediately."

SURPRISED to find himself on a university campus, the man began to wonder if he was in the right place.

Dr. Elizabeth Simmonds, vice-president of the alumni association, immediately put her visitor at ease. "I understand you are interested in learning what many of us have learned from The One Minute Sales Person. To tell you the truth, I only learned about it a few years ago myself. Until then, I never thought of myself as being able to sell anything."

She explained that she used her selling skills to help her succeed in three areas at the college. As an administrator, she helped other faculty members feel a pride in having a well-run department. As a teacher, she helped her students gain the best in artistic knowledge and skills. And now as a director of the major fund-raising group, she raised millions of dollars every year by helping alumni and other contributors feel they owned a part of a university they'd like to be associated with.

The amazed man was eager to get to the answers. "Can you tell me what you actually *do* when you sell?"

The woman felt a little uncomfortable talking about selling to a sales person. But then she had learned from The One Minute Sales Person himself.

"Let me begin," she suggested, "by turning the tables on you for just a moment. What do you usually do *before* a sale?"

"Before? Well, I try to find out something about the company and the person I'm calling on."

"I know that's very important and useful," Dr. Simmonds said, "but what's on your mind during that minute just before you get face to face with the other person?"

"Well, often I go over objections that might come up and things that could go wrong."

"So when you think of it," she said, "you paint a mental picture in your mind of what will happen before it happens. What you've just told me is that you think about what could go wrong."

She smiled and said, "Boy, does that sound familiar! That's what I used to do just before I went into a faculty meeting—or a fund-raising event. I thought I was being practical and I was trying to be well prepared. But all I got were disappointing results.

"Now, before I start to help anybody buy anything, I take a minute (and that's about all it takes) to see the entire encounter running smoothly from beginning to end. I call this process The One Minute Rehearsal."

"You see it *all* in only one minute?"

"All the important parts. Take a look at television commercials that appeal to you. The best ones manage to identify with your problem and then make both you and the advertiser look great for getting together—all in a minute or less. A good One Minute Rehearsal looks a lot like that—especially like the fun commercials.

"The more upbeat and positive your One Minute Rehearsal, the more likely your success. In fact:

*

Whenever I am successful

I know I have chosen,
consciously or unconsciously,

to use
the positive thoughts
that created my success.

*

"When you see a television commercial, think about the enjoyable problem solving you see," the woman added.

Then she smiled and said, "What have you been choosing to see lately?"

The man looked sheepish and then laughed at himself. "I guess I look at what might go wrong."

"Sure, and guess what happens?"

"Things go wrong," the visitor laughed.

Then he said, "You know, now that I think of it, I used to see selling as enjoyable. And I made a lot more sales.

"Tell me this," he said, "when you see these mental images before a sale, are they visual—like seeing the TV commercials you were talking about?"

"Actually, mine are radio commercials," said Dr. Simmonds. "I think in words. But other people I know do 'see' themselves succeeding. The One Minute Sales Person says, 'The best people use whatever works best for them.'"

"When I did it best," the man reflected, "I would recall a past selling success in my mind and then emulate that on my next call."

"You see," the woman pointed out, "you already know. You've already done it successfully on occasion. You're like all the rest of us. It's just a question of investing a minute or so to do it! That's why it's called One Minute Selling. It's fast and it works."

When the man wanted to know more about The Rehearsal, she spelled it out in three parts:

"The first part," she explained, "is A Walk in the Other Person's Shoes—seeing things from his side. The second part is The Advantages—how the features of my product combine to solve his problem. And the third part, as corny as it may sound, is The Happy Ending—seeing the other person using and benefiting from what he buys— and feeling good about it."

"Would you explain each one of these?"

The sales person said, "I don't mean to be rude, but no, I won't." Then she smiled and added, "At least not to your immediate satisfaction. No one can ever learn fully through someone else's explanation—but sometimes a hint or two can help us pull the answers from within, or figure things out for ourselves."

"So that's what The One Minute Sales Person was up to with me," the visitor realized. "Instead of *telling* me about Purpose, he drew it all out of me!"

"But he couldn't have done it if you didn't already 'know,'" she pointed out. "Let's try you again with The One Minute Rehearsal. How, for example, do you think you could take A Walk in the Other Person's Shoes?"

"I suppose," he began, "I could just remember how I feel when I am the buyer. Ironically, I tend to distrust people who are selling me. And I want good value for the money I spend. I want to be able to count on the person I am buying from for service if I need it."

Elizabeth Simmonds smiled and said, "You see! You just did what the best sales people know:

*

*Before I can walk
in another person's shoes,*

*I must first
take off my own.*

*

"You just took off your seller shoes and put on your buyer shoes. Once you've done that, it makes every sale easier. It's like parents who successfully sell their ideas to their children because they also take a minute to see things from their children's point of view.

"The second part of The Rehearsal is almost as easy—especially if you have done your homework on the service, product, or idea you are selling. If you've been smart enough to study and keep up on the latest features of what you have to offer, you can quickly review The Advantages—how they can be applied to the other person's advantage."

"And the third part of The One Minute Rehearsal?" the man asked. "The Happy Ending?"

"How would *you* see the third part?" she asked.

"That would vary," the man said, "depending on who was buying what from me."

"Exactly," Dr. Simmonds agreed. "I see it differently in my own mind if I am helping a student buy an idea or an alumnus make a financial contribution."

"You know," said her visitor, "I think I'm beginning to get how The One Minute Rehearsal works. While you were talking, I was mentally seeing an important client I'll be calling on soon. I saw her needs from *her* viewpoint. I saw the practical advantages to her of what I am representing. And I saw her buying and benefiting from using it—and feeling good about it.

"I was beginning to feel the energy—the power—of helping the other person get the feelings she wants. Is that a common reaction?"

"Yes, it is. We use a lot of words to describe that feeling—words like 'confidence,' 'courage,' 'a winning attitude.' That's the feeling that fuels high performance and ensures better results.

"But remember, the worrisome images we create and play in our minds are just as powerful. These are the images that create fear and doubt.

"The exciting reality is that we can create and play the mental movies of our *choice*. That's power.

"Most sales people (the eighty percent who make only twenty percent of the sales) are not aware of the negative images they are seeing in their minds just before they make a sales call. They're not aware of the power such images have to undermine sales.

"You, however, can be part of the outstanding twenty percent of sales people who make eighty percent of the sales. You can choose your success by 'seeing' it before it happens."

"I think I'll take note when I watch effective television commercials!" the man said enthusiastically.

"But don't forget," Dr. Simmonds cautioned, "the key hero of your Rehearsal is the *other* person. The more you see yourself focusing on what *he* wants, the more quickly you will help him buy."

It seemed as if the man had just arrived and yet he was already writing down a summary of what he had learned, thanking Dr. Simmonds, and leaving the university campus.

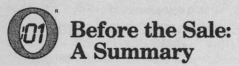

Before the Sale: A Summary

I remind myself that my purpose is to help other people feel good about what they bought and about themselves for buying.

Before each sale I help myself realize my purpose by using The One Minute Rehearsal, which helps me see what I want to have happen before it happens.

1. I mentally Walk in Other People's Shoes in order to help me see things from their point of view.

2. I mentally see The Advantages of my service, product, or idea and how these advantages can help other people get what they want.

3. I mentally see The Happy Ending for the other people. They *feel* the way they want to feel: good about what they bought and about themselves for buying.

I see myself getting what I want: more sales with less stress.

What I do before the sale is the first of three parts in the Game Plan for Selling to Others.

A brief summary of

THE ONE MINUTE SALES PERSON'S "GAME PLAN"
The Quickest Way to More Sales with Less Stress

I START
with
MY PURPOSE
I help people get the feelings <u>they</u> want—soon!

↓

SELLING TO OTHERS

↓

Before the Sale

- First, I see other people getting the feelings THEY want. Then I see me getting what I want.
- I study the features and advantages of what I sell—thoroughly and often.
- I see the benefits of what I sell actually helping others get the feelings they want.

During the Sale

-
-
-
-
-
-

After the Sale

-
-
-

THE man reflected on the wisdom he'd gained from the university administrator. It certainly confirmed his early thoughts that when people learn how to sell they can prosper in many different ways.

He was about to meet John Turnquist, one of the most successful sales people in insurance, earning an income of over one million dollars from selling.

But what was more impressive was that Turnquist was a well-respected gentleman who enjoyed his life, and was obviously at peace with himself and the world. He also had the time to enjoy other things in life besides financial success. It sounded familiar.

The man was eager to learn how to do the same with his own life. In the past, he would have been a little uncomfortable in the presence of someone as well known as John Turnquist. But he had mentally rehearsed for this meeting, had already "seen" the enjoyable outcome, and felt energized and confident.

As the two men shook hands, the visitor quickly shared with Turnquist his exciting learning experiences at the first two offices and let him know he was eager for more. "I never cared much for teachers before," he concluded, "but you people don't seem to teach so much as you help me like to learn!"

"*That*, my good man," Turnquist replied, "is the secret that makes selling so easy for me.

"I never forget that *people hate to be sold, but they love to buy*.

"When I'm at my best, I find that all I'm doing is helping people do what they already like to do: to feel good about what they buy."

"Well, I'd like to believe it's that simple. But I find that people resist *any* salesperson. I do it myself."

"What I hear you saying is that you hate to be sold. Who doesn't? When you feel you're being sold you question the intent of the other person and don't feel that you're in control of what's happening.

"Just the opposite is true when you know you're doing the *buying*. It's fun. You *enjoy* it. That happens when the sales person is clearly on your side and doesn't stray from what you want."

"I see what you mean. People buy for their reasons, not ours."

"Sure," Turnquist said. "That's why my sales approach is based on this:

*

*When I want to remember
how to sell,*

*I simply recall
how I—and other people—
like to buy.*

*

"Do you know The One Minute Rehearsal?"

"Yes. In fact, I did one myself right before I came in here today." It felt good.

"What you accomplish in that One Minute Rehearsal *before* the sale simplifies your job *during* the sale. All you have to do is help the other person share the image you've already created—to *his* advantage!"

"Let's see if I read you right," said the man, by now realizing he could find his own answers. "It's up to me during the sale to help the other people see the 'commercial' that I had them starring in— recognizing their problem, seeing my product in action to solve it, and thereafter enjoying the good feelings they want."

"Yes. But remember, beforehand you can at best *anticipate* their needs and the feelings they want. During the process you have a chance to adapt your vision to *their* reasons for buying."

"What *are* their reasons?"

"Those, of course, are different for every customer. Before we see their reasons for buying, let's look at the four common reasons for their *not* buying—the four obstacles to their not getting what they want.

"Sales people exist to help buyers buy. But if buyers don't *trust* the sales person, don't feel a *need* for our service, don't believe the product offers more *help* than a competitor's, and aren't in any *hurry* to buy, they won't accept our assistance."

"So how do we help them overcome the obstacles?"

"To help people feel *trust*, I remember my purpose. People can soon sense it when your purpose is to help them. I tell the person I am going to do something and I do it either during that sales call or by the time I call again. And I describe *Purpose, Process, Payoff.*"

"Is that like the purpose in Selling On Purpose?"

"Yes. Once you know your purpose, it's up to you to *communicate* it to the other person. If I were calling on you, it might sound like this:

"'Sir, in thinking about this call it occurred to me that most of the people I've worked with in the past have had some questions they wanted answered before we ever got started. They wanted to know the *purpose* of our getting together, the *process* they could expect if they chose to look into our service, and finally their *payoff* for the time they might invest with me. If those questions have crossed your mind, I'd like to answer them.' Does that sound all right?"

"Yes. Let me hear your answer!"

"Well, my answer is . . ." Turnquist stopped and laughed. "It's not my answer that's important. It's the process that helped you want to hear more."

"Well, it sounds like most people would at least be willing to take the next step. And I suppose that's all you can expect since trust isn't something that you can earn in a sentence or two! How will you know if you're earning their trust?"

"By how willing they are to share their situation with you. That's moving into the next process, which deals with the 'no need' obstacle.

"One of the most helpful values we provide is helping people recognize what *they* really want.

"We do that with our ability to ask relevant questions and use intense listening."

"Can you give me an example of both?"

"That's easy. I ask 'have' questions like 'What do you like most about what you already have?' And then 'want' questions like 'What do you want that you don't have?' 'Would it be fair to ask what you like least about what you've got?' And so on.

"This is where good listening and good feedback come in. If you listen closely to their answers, you'll be able to hear whether there is any difference between what they have now and what they want—which adds up to how they'd like to be feeling.

"Then I take a minute to summarize the key points, repeating them back to let them know I've listened and understood. Most important, I very clearly point out the difference between what they've got and what they want, so they can recognize their problem and discover the feelings they want."

"Why is *that* so important?"

"That makes everything else that follows easier. Have you ever presented a solution to a problem that someone didn't feel he had?"

"Yes, and it's frustrating."

"Compare that with saying, 'Sir, based upon what you told me about so-and-so [his needs], I'd like to suggest such-and-such [my product service or idea].' That's how problems and solutions are tied together."

"How about when they've recognized a need, but I'm in competition with another product—should I knock the competition, or compare it to my product?"

"How do you feel," the successful sales person asked, "when somebody else knocks the competition?"

"Sometimes I lose respect for the sales person. And I lose a little trust."

"Me too. So I don't do it. My answer is to tell them about another person, much like themselves, who benefited from buying what I have to offer—if indeed that was honestly the case.

"Here is where, if appropriate, I can point out the unique advantages of what I have to offer, and how they worked on that other person's similar problem. But the one thing I want to be sure to include is mention of the specific feelings my customer wants and that another person experienced—the satisfaction, the reduced anxiety, the newfound security—whatever it is that my *present* customer actually wants to buy."

"What do you mean?"

"If you're going to be selling, you'd better know what it is that people really buy."

"Okay, what is it people really buy?"

*

*People don't buy
our services, products, or ideas.*

*They buy how they imagine
using them will make them
<u>feel</u>.*

*

"I used to sell radial tires before I sold insurance," Turnquist began, "and I sold more tires than anyone."

The visitor interrupted with a smile. "And you did it in less time than the other sales people."

Turnquist laughed, "How did you guess?

"I once called on a trucking account. The competition for the order was fierce.

"But I noticed the buyer's family photographs on his desk. We began talking about life and it was obvious that we both cared about family life. He talked about his truck drivers and how often they were away from their families and what would happen to their families if anything happened to them.

"Then I presented the safety features of our radial tires. Everyone else was featuring mileage and economy. Guess who got the big contract?"

"I see. So you took the few extra minutes to listen to what the buyer was really interested in— safety—instead of going in and pitching what you thought was important about your product."

"Yes. Find out what the other person wants."

"What if you can't find out?" the man asked.

"I do two things. First, I ask more questions and listen more intently. Usually, by investing the extra few minutes, I discover the needs."

"And if you don't?" the man asked.

"If he feels he doesn't have a need, I get out of the person's office. I never create a need, since that is not in the other person's best interest. It would also rob me of eighty percent of my time and get only twenty percent of my results.

"The fastest way to sell is to honestly help people see how it's really in their best interests. Then *they* will act—and they will act *quickly*.

"If it is not, I refer them to the best source I know and get on to the next person I can really help. I don't waste time kidding myself or the other person."

"Okay," the visitor summed up, "let's say they trust me, feel a need, and see that I can help them meet their need and get the feelings they want. What could possibly keep them from taking action now?"

"Sometimes you just have to ask. You'd be surprised at how many sales people are afraid to ask for action."

The man groaned, recalling the many sales he had let slip away for just that reason.

"Usually, however, it's the other person's fear that is the cause of 'no hurry.' The idea then is to suggest a course of action that will result in maximum opportunity for them to gain with the minimum risk.

"Sales people do this every day by providing a money-back guarantee, a free trial period, a small sample or small step to see how it works before jumping in completely. When the smallest personal risk is combined with the greatest personal payoff, people get over 'no hurry' in a hurry."

The visitor took out his notebook and briefly summarized what he had heard—as though he had already begun to use it himself:

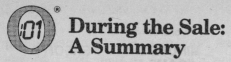

During the Sale: A Summary

1. I take a minute to remind myself of my purpose: to help people get the good feelings they want—about what they bought and about themselves for buying.

2. I remind myself of my strategy: to help the other person see and feel what I had envisioned in my One Minute Rehearsal, which I modify during the process according to what the other person wants.

3. I recall obstacles people have to getting what *they* want: no trust, no need, no help, no hurry.

4. I help establish trust with people by Selling On Purpose, doing what I say I will do, and describing my *purpose*, our sales *process*, and their *payoff*.

5. To discover their needs, I ask 'have' questions and 'want' questions. The difference is our opportunity—theirs and mine, in that order.

6. I listen. Then I take a minute to summarize what I have heard—to show I understand.

7. Based on what *they* feel they want, I help them get it. If I can't help, I tell them and help them get their payoffs by recommending someone who *can* help.

8. If I can help, I tell them about someone like themselves whom I helped get what he wanted.

9. When they see that they can get what they want, I show them how they can get it with the least personal risk and the greatest personal payoff.

10. I ask them to buy.

What I do during the sale is the second of three parts in the Game Plan for Selling to Others:

A brief summary of

THE ONE MINUTE SALES PERSON'S "GAME PLAN"
The Quickest Way to More Sales with Less Stress

I START
with

MY PURPOSE
I help people get the feelings <u>they</u> want—soon!

SELLING TO OTHERS

Before the Sale

- First, I see other people getting the feelings THEY want. Then I see me getting what I want.
- I study the features and advantages of what I sell—thoroughly and often.
- I see the benefits of what I sell actually helping others get the feelings they want.

During the Sale

- I sell the way I and the other person like to buy. I invest time as a PERSON.
- I ask "have" questions and "want" questions.
- The difference is the problem.
- I listen and I repeat back what I have heard.
- I honestly relate my service, product, or idea only to what <u>the other person</u> wants to feel.
- The other person closes the sale when he sees he gets the maximum benefits with the minimum personal risk.

After the Sale

-
-
-

TODAY he was meeting Diane Rosini. The One Minute Sales Person had told him that Rosini was the most successful sales person he'd ever known at getting the most done with the least amount of effort.

She was a very professional sales person. Her secret, he had said, was her ability to get other people to refer many other buyers to her. She spent very little time cold-calling. She spent most of her time taking orders from people who wanted to buy specifically from her. That got his attention.

Sitting across from Rosini confirmed one thing: She certainly seemed relaxed. She seemed to have all the time in the world.

The man asked, "What is your secret?"

She said, "For me, the key minutes in a sale and the most important work I do come after people buy from me. These minutes pay the highest rewards.

"Do you know," she asked, "that the majority of sales people seldom contact the people they've helped, after the sale has been made?"

The man responded, "No. Come to think of it, I don't contact most of the people I sell afterward either, unless of course there's a problem."

"Did you ever wonder why?" the woman asked.

"I've found that most of the time sales people don't like to contact their customers, just because they're afraid there might be a problem."

"It's the 'no news is good news' syndrome," said Rosini.

"What's happening is that the majority of people who buy something, from baby buggies to battleships, are not used to being contacted after the sale. What I'm going to tell you now seems to be the best-kept secret I know among sales people."

*

*After I sell On Purpose,
people feel good*

*about what they bought
and about themselves.*

*And so they give me invaluable
REFERRALS!*

*

"So people don't just do it for you, but because it makes them feel good to help their friends. People do things for their reasons, not ours. It sounds so simple!"

She smiled. "Success is doing the simple well."

"I think that most sales people don't follow up after the sale," she volunteered, "because they're afraid they'll hear bad news. Let me explain.

"After people have bought, I telephone them several times. I let them know that the purpose of my calls is to find out if they are enjoying and benefiting from using what they bought from me.

"If they are, I honestly and briefly praise them for their buying decision. I remind them of something specific they did during the sales process that helped them make such a good decision.

"I keep a simple file on every customer that includes that kind of information. After I've praised them, I tell them about a gift that I'm sending them. Usually it's an inexpensive feature they could have bought but didn't—one that has added value.

"It's a means of doing something beyond what they expected. For most people, the phone calls and praisings are enough, and investing these brief minutes after the sale keeps me on purpose.

"Then I ask them if they know other people who would appreciate my help. Most people are more than happy to oblige. When I take good care of customers, they take good care of me—with referrals galore!"

"What if the news is bad after the sale and things aren't working? What do you do then?"

"First, I don't see it as bad news. That's something we create in our heads. It's only information.

"My experience is that any information I get gives me an opportunity to help, to provide added value with service. And most people are fair.

"They know that sometimes things get off track. But usually their past experience in these situations is that nobody seems to care. So they're surprised when I jump in and am excited about the opportunity to help. These bad experiences usually provide my best referrals later. And they often lead to repeat business.

"That's why it's so easy for me to get excited and stay excited even when things are going wrong."

"When I came in here," the man noted, "I saw how relaxed you were. And now I hear your excitement when you talk about helping your customers.

"That's a nice combination—relaxed excitement.

"And why not? You have all those people out there thanking you by giving you referrals. It's as if they are working for you, for free. That's what I call making more sales with less stress."

He took note of what he had learned:

After the Sale: A Summary

After each sale I continue to Sell On Purpose: to have people feel good about what they bought and about themselves for buying.

1. I contact people after the sale to be sure that people are feeling good about what they bought and about themselves for buying.

2. If they are not happy, I take the opportunity to help make things right for the other person.

3. When they are pleased, I praise their buying decision and specifically point out something they did that helped that action come about.

4. I exceed their expectations by providing some form of added value.

5. When they are feeling good, I ask people for active referrals. I ask for the names of people they know whom I can contact, using the buyer's name as a recommendation.

What I do after the sale is the third part of an overall Game Plan for Selling to Others:

A brief summary of

THE ONE MINUTE SALES PERSON'S "GAME PLAN"
The Quickest Way to More Sales with Less Stress

I START
with

MY PURPOSE
I help people get the feelings <u>they</u> want—soon!

SELLING TO OTHERS

Before the Sale

- First, I see other people getting the feelings THEY want. Then I see me getting what I want.
- I study the features and advantages of what I sell—thoroughly and often.
- I see the benefits of what I sell actually helping others get the feelings they want.

During the Sale

- I sell the way I and the other person like to buy. I invest time as a PERSON.
- I ask "have" questions and "want" questions.
- The difference is the problem.
- I listen and I repeat back what I have heard.
- I honestly relate my service, product, or idea only to what <u>the other person</u> wants to feel.
- The other person closes the sale when he sees he gets the maximum benefits with the minimum personal risk.

After the Sale

- I frequently follow up to make sure people are actually feeling good about owning what they bought from me.
- If there is a problem, I help them solve it—and thus strengthen our relationship.
- When they are feeling good about what they bought, I ask for <u>active</u> referrals.

SALES Manager David Schmidt came around from behind his desk and shook hands with the man.

When the visitor mentioned how unusual he found many of the sales people he had met, the sales manager admitted that he didn't want to be like a lot of other sales managers either. "I don't want to be like the Canadian hunting dog."

When the visitor voiced his confusion, the manager smiled and said, "This American went hunting in Canada. He was lucky because he was given the best dog to hunt with. The dog's name was Salesman."

The visitor smiled.

"For the first time in his life, the American got his full quota of birds in only two days. 'That's the greatest hunting dog I've ever seen,' he said to his Canadian host. 'I'd love to have him again next time.'

"But when the American returned the following year, he was disappointed. He was told that there was no use in his having Salesman this year.

"When he asked why, he was told, 'I'm afraid we made a very big mistake with that dog. We changed his name to Sales Manager.'

"The American asked, 'What possible difference could that make?'

"'It made a big difference,' he was told. 'Ever since he was named Sales Manager he just sits around all day on his tail and barks!'"

Both men laughed. The man was impressed by the way One Minute Sales People could laugh and not take themselves too seriously.

The sales manager made it clear that he wanted to be a great help to the sales people who worked with him. It wasn't long before he began to explain the second part of One Minute Selling.

"The first half, Selling to Others," he said, "is taking good care of the *customer*. The second part, Selling to Me, is taking good care of the *sales person*.

"But as good as it is for the customer and for the sales person," the sales manager added, "do you know what I like best about it?"

Without waiting he said, "I like the second half of One Minute Selling—the self-management half—because it makes my job a lot easier. When people are managing themselves, it saves me time and energy—and there is less personnel turnover."

"Why less turnover?" the visitor asked.

"Because our sales people like it," the sales manager said. "It's a great way for them to take good care of themselves. When the people in my department take just as good care of *themselves* as they do of their customers, they make more sales more easily—and thus they enjoy working here more.

"As you know," the outstanding sales manager said, "sales people are in the field selling and are not under the scrutiny of an office manager. Sales people like this. One of the reasons many of them went into sales is because they like being their own boss. It makes them feel good.

"In fact, Self-Managed Selling realizes that the better people feel about themselves, the better job they do. It is based on just this: *Sales people who feel good about themselves produce good results.*

"The very best managers," Schmidt continued, "are discovering that people feel best about themselves at work when they *want* to do something—not when they *have* to do something.

"When people see that they are doing something for themselves, they are more apt to actually do it—and without being constantly managed."

The visitor said, "That's like the first half of One Minute Selling. When the other person feels he's getting what he *wants*—to feel good about what he's buying, and about himself for buying—he's more apt to do it."

The same method of selling to others can be used in selling you to you. It's a very powerful parallel."

"How do you, as a sales manager, help your sales people do this?"

"Before we talk about how we do it," the manager cautioned, "let's look at the basic source of power for each individual sales person who uses Self-Managed Selling. It is simply this:

*

Self-Managed Selling

*first helps me realize
how good I <u>already</u> am*

*and then it lets me enjoy
becoming even <u>better</u>!*

*

"The most powerful fuel for high personal performance in selling is high *self-esteem*.

"You asked how I help our sales people feel good about themselves. Well, I first began by becoming a One Minute Manager. By that I mean that I used three effective management methods: I set One Minute Goals, gave One Minute Praisings, and applied One Minute Reprimands. And I got very good results.

"But I knew that sales people were unique. They were out in the world selling and needed to be their own managers. But they wanted some practical help from me.

"So I adapted these methods for my sales people into One Minute Self-Management. Once they learned to use it, they loved it because it gives them what they want—control over their own lives."

"How do they use the three methods?"

The manager responded, "Why don't you ask them?"

The visitor was amazed at how confident everyone was. It seemed that the more you were allowed to probe and question the value of One Minute Selling through the people who used it, the more apparent its value became.

The man thanked the exceptional sales manager for his help and left to meet with some of these "extraordinary" sales people.

He was already looking forward to the possibility of getting the same great results for himself.

"**A**CCOUNTING for sales is now more important in every business," the man heard from the woman accountant he had just met. "Even doctors and lawyers are now marketing and advertising their services."

Because she was bringing in many new accounts, Carolyn Stafford, CPA, was on the way to becoming a senior partner in a prestigious accounting firm. She knew how to use the three secrets of Self-Managed Selling.

"Our office manager tells me you want to know more about the first secret: One Minute Goals.

"Since David Schmidt told my manager about it and he taught me, I have almost doubled the number of new clients I have been able to bring into our firm. As an accountant, I never thought I'd like to sell or that I'd be able to sell. But it has helped me prosper. And I even enjoy my job more."

"I gather then that you appreciate your sales manager. Am I right?"

"I think he is an exceptional manager," she answered, "because he helped me learn how to manage myself."

"Specifically, what *are* One Minute Goals and just how do they help you in Self-Managed Selling?"

"They are goals I can often 'see' in my mind—in only a minute. You'll see why that's important later.

"I do four specific things: 1.) I decide on 'the few, important twenty percent'—and they become my goals. 2.) I write my goals down in a special way. 3.) I often review my goals. 4.) I frequently look at my goals and then at my *behavior* to see if it matches my goals."

The man took out his notebook to record what he sensed was going to be useful information. "Could you please explain more about each of the things you do?"

"Yes. Like other One Minute Sales People, I've learned that about twenty percent of what I do during the day gives me about eighty percent of my payoff.

"So the *first* thing I do is sort out what that important twenty percent is, and then I concentrate only on that. I choose not to do the eighty percent—the unnecessary.

"I do less work, so I am less tired. Thus I have the energy and concentration to do important things well."

"Could you give me a practical example of how you use this technique?"

"A good example of this twenty/eighty law is analyzing my sales accounts. When I look closely, I realize that about twenty percent of my accounts give me and my company about eighty percent of our cash flow. So I concentrate on doing an outstanding job on this twenty percent.

"Then I set it up so that the other eighty percent of potential accounts who hear about the great job I am doing with the key twenty percent contact me to get the same benefits. It's efficient because they come to me."

"What do you do on the key twenty percent?" the visitor asked.

"After I decide who the twenty percent are, the *second* thing I do is to write down *specifically* whatever I would like to see happen for me. I write out these key goals in two parts: what I am *doing* and how I *feel*. I write it in the first person, present tense—as though it is already real. *I am doing . . . And I am feeling . . .*

"Is that all there is to it?" the man asked.

"Not quite. To let me more easily *feel* that my goal has already come true, I dress it up with words that help me feel the advantages for myself. And that is the critical thing—my *feeling* that it is already true."

The sales person asked the young woman, "Can you give me a general example?"

"Sure. A friend of mine had a personal goal recently to own a boat. But he wasn't sure he had the time or the money ever to realize it. After learning about the power of One Minute Goals, he wrote his goal out so he could actually *feel* it as already realized.

"He wrote out on a card and 'saw' something like this:

It is August of next year and I own a 32-foot blue and white sailboat that sleeps six. I am wearing my favorite cap and shoes while I enjoy fishing, the feel of the sun on my face, and the joy of having my best friends on board.

The man smiled. "I feel like I'm on the boat."

"That's the idea," the woman confirmed, "to feel it's already happening. My friend mentally 'saw' his goal by frequently reviewing it in his mind as he read and reread his goal—over and over.

"Then the funniest thing happened.

"Without a lot of extra effort, that year he got his boat. It didn't happen exactly when or how he thought it would. It seldom does. But it happened! In fact, it happened sooner and more easily than he had hoped.

"I—and others—who have used One Minute Goals have found the same thing," Stafford added. "We now realize more of our goals more often and with less stress.

"The power of One Minute Goals—which frankly I do not fully understand, but have certainly observed—seems to come from this apparently universal truth:

*

We become

what we
think about.

*

The man recalled, "That's like a basketball coach I heard of who divided his team into two groups to see which could most improve its free-throw shooting. One group practiced shooting every day while the other group practiced for the same amount of time—only in their mind's eye. They just saw their shots going into the basket one hundred percent of the time. They saw themselves winning.

"When the two groups competed, those who thought about scoring points more often did indeed outscore their teammates. We become what we think about!"

"That's a great example," the woman said.

The man thought for a moment, then remarked, "That's like The One Minute Sales Rehearsal we use before the sale. We help the other person get what he wants—by seeing him first in our own mind, already feeling good about getting what he wanted.

"One Minute Goals," the man noted enthusiastically, "are based on the same psychological principles. They just help us get what *we* want."

"You're a quick study," Stafford said. "You just said what I was going to tell you—that selling others and selling yourself are very much alike. In fact, you just proved what The One Minute Sales Person says: 'We all have all of the answers within us, if we just listen to ourselves.'"

The man missed the point. He asked, "How, specifically, do you use One Minute Goals in selling?"

"I use it in two ways: generally and specifically."

"On one five-by-seven card, I long ago wrote out, in detail, the general principles I want to keep in mind—before, during, and after every sales call I make. This *general card* has the three parts of The Rehearsal before the sale, the key things I do during the sale, and the follow-up steps I do after the sale."

"Then how do you use it specifically?"

"Then I create my *specific cards*. I quickly write out my sales goals for each account I am going after on a smaller three-by-five card. It takes me only a few minutes to do this but it really helps me focus in.

"My sales goals vary, but my use of this quick and powerful technique is pretty much the same."

"What do you do next?" the visitor wanted to know.

"After I decide what is important and have written out my goals in a way that lets me feel they have already happened for me, the *third* thing I do is to read and reread my key goals over and over again—even if I think I already know my goals.

"It may sound mechanical to you," Stafford said, "to read and reread your goals, but if you want to change anything, even a belief, you really can—easily."

"How?" the man asked.

"How do *you* think you could do it?" The successful young woman had learned well from her sales manager.

"I could write out my goals on a card and carry the card in my wallet. Then, whenever I had time to kill, I could read and reread my goals—so that I see them as already being realized."

He added, "Maybe I could paste a card up next to my shaving mirror or put one next to my bed to read when I wake up and before I go to sleep."

Stafford said, "Whatever *you* think will work is the way to do it. As The One Minute Sales Person tells us, 'Do it your own way and it will probably work for you; do it someone else's way and it probably won't.'

"You've already discovered that you have all the answers inside you. I know I'm glad my manager helped me discover it for myself because I now realize that we all do. And you've just demonstrated it.

"I'm just learning that the more I know what I want to do, the more I can figure out *how* to do it myself."

The visitor felt good. He was beginning to think maybe he could dramatically improve the way he was selling. Maybe with the use of One Minute Goals, he could learn how to make more sales with less stress—soon.

"Can you give me another example of what you are talking about—one related to sales?"

"Yes. Let's say you want to increase your sales. You might write down your goal this way: *I am increasing my sales by three percent this month and I am enjoying the recognition and rewards that come along with this—including making more money and feeling more peaceful.*

The man commented, "Three percent doesn't seem like much. Would that be a high enough goal to set?"

"A month?" the young woman asked. "Think about it."

The man did and then realized, "If I kept increasing my sales by three percent each month, I'd increase my sales by over thirty-five percent a year, wouldn't I?"

"Practically," the young woman said.

"What about the *fourth* thing you do?" the man asked. "You said you compared your behavior with your goals. How do you do it?"

"It's very easy. I have a One Minute Sales Person Calendar that I use." The accountant leaned across the desk and handed it to the man.

"Look at the column on the left side of the page. See how it lists my business and my personal goals. At the top of the goal column it says *twenty percent get eighty percent*

"Now look at what is at the very center of the calendar each month: *I look at my goals. I look at my behavior (e.g., my appointments). I see if my behavior matches my goals.*

"This looks fantastic," the man said with enthusiasm. "It could be a big help."

"It is. But remember," she cautioned, "the calendar works only when you *use* it."

The man smiled and said, "That is true of everything, isn't it? We know a good deal, but we don't always *use* what we know."

The successful woman responded, "That is the beauty of the One Minute Selling System. It reminds me of what I know works—with other people and with myself.

"And it's so simple, I can *use* it.

"I never thought I could be good at selling," Stafford added. "But knowing how to do something as simple as using this powerful One Minute Goal Setting daily, I'm beginning to realize that I can do almost anything."

The man said, "Thanks to you and all the other One Minute Sales People, I'm beginning to think I can too."

Before he left to meet with Leon Williams later that afternoon, the visitor wrote down what he had learned, as though he were already doing it.

⓪1 My Sales Goals: A Summary

One Minute Goals work well for me when:

1. I focus only on what is important—*the 20% of what I do* (my key goals) that gets me *80%* of my results.

2. I write, on a single sheet of paper in 250 words or less, my key sales goals—*specifically,* what I want and how good it feels to have it—in the first person, present tense so that I can *feel* myself already realizing my goals. *I am doing . . . I feel . . .*

3. I take a minute to read and reread my goals frequently, knowing that repetition will lead to change.

4. I take a minute every now and then to look at my goals and then I look at my behavior (for example, my appointments). I see if my behavior matches my goals.

I remind myself that the more *often* I do this, the more I manage—on my own—to achieve my sales goals and to get what I want: to feel good about what I do and to feel good about myself.

My One Minute Goals are the first of three parts in the overall Game Plan for Selling to Me.

A brief summary of

THE ONE MINUTE SALES PERSON'S "GAME PLAN"
The Quickest Way to More Sales with Less Stress

I START
with

MY PURPOSE
I help people get the feelings <u>they</u> want—soon!

SELLING TO ME

My One Minute Goals

- I write out my goals on a single piece of paper in 250 words or less, as though they were already real.
- I read/reread them in only one minute.
- Each time I reread my goals, I see them as already achieved.

Goals (Even Partly) Achieved

> ### I WIN

-
-
-
-

Goals Not Achieved
(review goals)

> ### I LOSE

-
-
-
-
-

"**R**IGHT**," Leon Williams said shortly after he met the man. "A lot of sales managers are interested in sales people having determination and perseverance as part of their working style. But only the best ones know where those things come from."

"Where is that?" the visitor wanted to know.

"Inside the sales person," the successful Williams said. "That's the reason for self-management. It's not just to help you use your time well, although that is important. It's to bring out the best in yourself—all by yourself. The good news is that it is much easier to do than most people realize—and it takes only a minute."

"How do you do it?" the man wanted to know.

"Let me give you a useful overview. The self-management system is based on this: *Goals begin behaviors. Consequences maintain behaviors.*"

The visitor said, "I know about One Minute Goals."

Williams offered, "As powerful as goals are, I'll tell you something that is even more powerful."

The visitor took out his notebook.

"Self-Managed Selling," Williams said, "is based on the obvious fact that people who feel good about themselves produce good sales results."

"I know that's true with me," the visitor said. "The better I feel about myself, the better I work."

"You and everyone else - on this planet," Williams said. "The *second* secret of self-management," he began . . .

Just then, the man noticed the plaque on Leon Williams's desk. It said:

*

*I help myself realize
my sales goals*

*by catching myself
doing something
RIGHT!*

*

At first the visitor laughed, and then he thought and said, "I'm afraid I spend too much of my time catching myself doing something wrong. Like thinking of what I could have said during the sale but failed to, or how I should be making more cold calls, or . . ."

Williams interrupted him, "You're a lot like the rest of us, aren't you?" Both men smiled.

The visitor asked, "So, how do you catch yourself doing something right?"

The successful salesman said, "That is the second secret to Self-Managed Selling. Every now and then I give myself a *One Minute Praising.*"

"A what?" the man asked.

"It's very simple," Williams began.

By now the visitor had grown used to hearing that. "I'm sure it is," he said with a smile. "Can you tell me how you do it?"

"Certainly," the very successful sales person replied. "As long as you realize . . ."

"I know," the visitor interrupted, "as long as I realize that this is your way and that my way may be a bit different. We all need to learn how to sell with our own style—whatever makes sense to us."

Williams laughed and said, "I can see you've been talking to other One Minute Sales People. That's great. And that's right. Use the principles any way you see fit."

"I will," the man said. "Can you give me the principles of a One Minute Praising?"

"The main thing I do," Williams began, "is to *look* often during the day for the things I am doing that help me make more sales—with less stress.

"When I notice something I am doing right— like making a cold call or writing a follow-up letter—I catch myself. Then I take a minute to praise myself.

"I spend the first half minute or so on my *behavior* and the last half on my *self*.

"As soon as I realize I've done something I like, I tell myself specifically what I did right."

"Then I tell myself how good I feel about what I have just done—even if it's something that seems small to someone else. If I like it, I like it!

"Then I pause for a few seconds of silence— which seems like a long time when I do it—to let myself *feel* how good I feel about what I did. This feeling is what it is all about. You don't want to just think well of what you have done, you want to *feel good* about it. That's where the power is—in the feeling!

"Then in the next half minute or so (after I have thought about my *good behavior*) I think about my *good self*—the best part of who I feel I am.

"I remind myself that I am a good person. And that even with my human faults I basically like who *I am*."

Then Williams laughed and said, "I'm sure glad The One Minute Sales Person told me about One Minute Praisings. I'm not only feeling better, but I'm making a ton more money!"

The visitor laughed too. Then he summarized One Minute Praisings as something to use for himself:

(01)® My Praisings: A Summary

The One Minute Praising works well for me because I take a minute to have some fun once in a while and give myself some "sales recognition."

the first half of my praising

1. I catch myself doing something *right!*

2. I do not wait until I do something completely right—like making the sale. I go ahead and enjoy myself doing something *approximately right.*

3. I tell myself *specifically* what I *did.*

4. I tell myself how good I *feel* about it.

5. I slow down for a few seconds of silence to let myself smile and actually *feel* how good I feel.

the second half of my praising

6. I remind myself that I am a worthwhile person and that I like my *self.* I let myself feel it.

7. I tell myself to do this more often. Because I know that when I feel better about myself I produce better sales results.

My One Minute Praisings are the second part in the overall Game Plan for Selling Me to Me.

A brief summary of

THE ONE MINUTE SALES PERSON'S "GAME PLAN"
The Quickest Way to More Sales with Less Stress

I START

with

MY PURPOSE
I help people get the feelings <u>they</u> want—soon!

SELLING TO ME

My One Minute Goals

- I write out my goals on a single piece of paper in 250 words or less, as though they were already real.
- I read/reread them in only one minute.
- Each time I reread my goals, I see them as already achieved.

Goals (Even Partly) Achieved

I WIN

My One Minute Praisings

- I frequently take a minute to give myself some "sales recognition."
- I catch myself doing something right! (or approximately right!)
- I laugh and enjoy telling myself what I did and how good I feel about it.
- I take the time to FEEL how good I feel about what I have done.
- I encourage myself to do this again.

Goals Not Achieved
(review goals)

I LOSE

-
-
-
-
-

"So little time," the man thought. "It takes so little time to do something as important as catching myself doing something right!

"I also spent so little time with Mr. Williams, and yet I learned something that could last me a lifetime." He'd already begun to catch himself doing something right. He enjoyed the surge of confidence and energy he felt.

He had his doubts about One Minute Selling— or about anything that took only a minute, for that matter. But the more often he took a minute to *do* what he was learning, the more favorably he saw it.

He wondered, "What does a One Minute Sales Person do when he is not happy with his sales behavior?"

As soon as he met his seventh supersuccessful sales person, Cheryl Bartel, he got his answer.

"That's when you introduce yourself to the third secret of Self-Managed Selling," she said. "It's called the *One Minute Reprimand*."

The visitor smiled and said, "It figures. Let me see if I can work this out."

Bartel could see the confidence in her visitor and knew that some of that was coming from what he had been learning in the last few days. She had felt the same surge shortly after learning a selling system that she could believe in and that she could easily use.

"I gather," the man said, "that when you do something bad you take a minute out to reprimand yourself. Is that it?" he asked.

"No, it is not." She handed him a small plaque.

*

*Whenever I see
that my sales behavior
is unacceptable to me,*

*I take a minute
to reprimand my behavior*

and to praise my self.

*

"Look at the difference," she suggested, "between what you said and what I've shown you."

As the man thought, the successful woman remembered when she was first learning about One Minute Selling. She had fallen into the same trap the man had just fallen into.

She thought, "How alike we all are."

To help her visitor see, she asked, "Do you remember what The One Minute Sales Person says about what people really buy? That they do not buy our service, product, or idea—that they buy how *good* they imagine they will *feel* when they are using them?"

"Yes," he said. "I remember especially the part about buying a feeling they wanted."

"Well, *feeling good* is the key to what we all want, including feeling good about ourselves. So when you give yourself a One Minute Reprimand, remember two things if you really want to improve your own behavior.

"You want to feel bad about your behavior and good about yourself.

"When you spoke earlier about reprimanding yourself for your bad behavior, you fell into two traps.

"You never reprimand your *self*. You reprimand only your behavior.

"And one other important difference—your behavior is not 'bad.' That is too judgmental and too tough on yourself. Bad in whose eyes?

"Do you want someone else to manage you?" she asked. "Or do you want to manage yourself?"

"I'd rather manage myself," the visitor said. "That's one of the reasons I got into sales. I like the freedom."

"Me too," she said. "And with our freedom comes our responsibility—to ourselves and to those who depend on us, including our company and our customers."

Bartel continued, "If you want to manage yourself, then first realize that your behavior is not bad. It is simply 'unacceptable' to you. Because *you* feel it is getting in the way of what you want: to make more sales with less stress."

Then she asked, "What do you think is the first thing you should do when you do something unacceptable?"

The man thought for some time and finally saw what then seemed obvious. "The first thing is to become aware of my own unacceptable behavior. To *see* it," he clarified.

"Excellent," she said. "And then?"

The successful saleswoman went on to ask the man a series of questions and he eventually led himself to his own answers.

Before long, he said, "You know, as I learn more about Self-Managed Selling, I can see that selling ourselves on ourselves is a lot like selling our services, products, and ideas to others."

"It certainly is," Bartel said.

The man wrote down what he had heard and what he thought of himself while listening to the successful saleswoman. Once again, he wrote it as though he were already using The One Minute Reprimand on himself and enjoying the benefits.

My Reprimands: A Summary

The One Minute Reprimand works well for me when I remind myself of my purpose and, when I see I am off purpose, I reprimand my behavior and praise my self.

the first half of the reprimand

1. I realize that I deserve to behave in a way that helps me make more sales with less stress.
2. As *soon* as I see that my sales behavior is unacceptable to me, I reprimand my behavior.
3. I tell myself what I did *wrong*. I am *specific*.
4. I tell myself how I *feel* about what I did.
5. I pause for a few quiet moments of silence with myself to let myself *feel* how I feel about the behavior that is unacceptable to me.

the second half of the reprimand

6. I remember that I am obviously not my recent sales behavior.
7. I tell myself that while I do not like my behavior, I do, nonetheless, like *myself*.
8. I remind myself that I will choose to change my own behavior when I *feel* bad about my behavior and good about myself.
9. I realize when my reprimand is over, it's over.
10. I laugh at my mistake and get on with enjoying both my work and myself!

My One Minute Reprimand is the third part in the overall Game Plan for Selling to Me.

A brief summary of

THE ONE MINUTE SALES PERSON'S "GAME PLAN"
The Quickest Way to More Sales with Less Stress

I START

with

MY PURPOSE
I help people get the feelings <u>they</u> want—soon!

SELLING TO ME

My One Minute Goals

- I write out my goals on a single piece of paper in 250 words or less, as though they were already real.
- I read/reread them in only one minute.
- Each time I reread my goals, I see them as already achieved.

Goals (Even Partly) Achieved

My One Minute Praisings

- I frequently take a minute to give myself some "sales recognition."
- I catch myself doing something right! (or approximately right!)
- I laugh and enjoy telling myself what I did and how good I feel about it.
- I take the time to FEEL how good I feel about what I have done.
- I encourage myself to do this again.

*Goals Not Achieved
(review goals)*

I LOSE

My One Minute Reprimands

- I reprimand my behavior when it is unacceptable to me.
- I specifically tell what I did wrong.
- I let myself FEEL how I feel about what I did (or did not do).
- I remember that I am not what I do.
- I am a valuable human being and I deserve the best behavior from me.
- I get off my back and back on purpose.

T HE One Minute Sales Person greeted the man with a warm smile and a strong handshake. "Well, what did you learn?"

"Well, it certainly seems to work for you," the man responded, "and for the others. But I'm still not sure. Maybe I might be able to use it successfully myself if I understood more about *why* it worked."

"That's true of all of us," The One Minute Sales Person said. "The more we understand about what we are doing, the more apt we are to do it.

"One Minute Selling works simply because it is the easiest and fastest way to help both buyer and seller feel the way they want to *feel*.

"Buyers want to feel good about what they bought and about themselves for buying.

"Similarly, sellers want to feel good about what they are doing to make a living and about themselves.

"The key to selling success is a working belief in the philosophy of Selling On Purpose. By a working belief, I mean you believe it enough to practice it daily.

"I remember Thomas Watson, IBM's founder and chairman of the board, saying that in order to survive and succeed, organizations and individuals must have *a sound set of beliefs* on which to base all policies and actions. To meet the challenges of a changing world, we must be prepared to change everything except these beliefs.

"He also added that the most important reason for his success was a 'respect for the individual.'

"One Minute Sales People have both these things: a belief in their purpose—*to help people feel good about what they bought and about themselves for buying*—and a respect for the individual.

"And the basis for this respect—for both the individual sales person and for the individual buyer is *integrity* and *honesty*."

The experienced sales person asked about the difference and was reminded that integrity is first telling the truth to yourself and honesty is then being truthful with other people.

"A One Minute Sales Person acts with integrity and honesty because it's the fastest way to get big results."

"That makes me think," the experienced sales person said, "of something I read about how Douglas Aircraft sold its first fleet of jets to Eastern Airlines.

"Donald Douglas was trained as an engineer at the Naval Academy and the Massachusetts Institute of Technology and he taught at MIT.

"Having established his own company, which became McDonnell Douglas, he wanted to get Eastern to purchase its first jet fleet from his company.

"However, like other people, this engineer had to be a successful sales person in order to get things done.

"He called on Eddie Rickenbacker, then president of Eastern Airlines. Rickenbacker told Douglas that his new DC-8 was competitive with Boeing's 707—with one very important exception: the noise-suppression system. Like Boeing's, the Douglas jet engines were too loud.

"Douglas was then given the chance to outpromise his competitor and perhaps get the contract. It was a very important sale to Douglas at the time."

"What did Douglas do?" The One Minute Sales Person wanted to know.

"After consulting with his fellow engineers, Douglas returned to say, 'In all honesty, I do not think I can make good on such a promise.'

"'Neither do I,' Rickenbacker said. 'But I was anxious to see if you were still honest with me.'

"Douglas had, in fact, built his company on a reputation for honesty. Then Douglas heard what he had hoped for. 'You have a contract for one hundred sixty-five million dollars. Now go and see what you can do about making those jet engines less noisy!'"

"That's a very practical example," The One Minute Sales Person commented. "It shows again how honesty is the most efficient way to help the other person buy.

"And how do you think Douglas felt about *himself* after that meeting?"

"I think his self-esteem was probably pretty high," the experienced sales person replied.

"Of course, and it is high self-esteem that fuels an exceptional performance in selling. What sells a product is the sales person's belief in himself."

"And when I have high self-esteem," the visitor said, "it insulates me from the inevitable low feeling that follows a rejection. I realize the customer is temporarily rejecting what I am selling. But he isn't rejecting me.

"And so I go on to my next sales call with energy and confidence. And the next person I call on can sense that and is more apt to do business with me."

"And it works," The One Minute Sales Person noted, "with products as large as an aircraft or as small as personal cosmetics; with services or with ideas.

"Another example can be found in the largest door-to-door cosmetics company in the world— Avon, which has an incredible one million four hundred thousand active sales representatives.

"One of the best sales people, in Avon's opinion, is a woman in Minnesota who says some of her most productive sales days are in blizzard conditions.

"She travels through the cold weather over icy roads to call on her clients, who tell her, 'Only you would come under such conditions.'

"They appreciate her. And they buy from her."

The experienced man said, "In other words, they know they can count on her!"

"Yes. That's the point. They trust her to look after them and their needs. They know she *cares*.

"As people see the world becoming more uncertain and more complicated, they need to be able to count on other people. And when they find someone they can trust, they do repeat business with them."

"I am beginning to understand why One Minute Selling can quickly help me make more *sales*.

"But how does the self-management part of One Minute Selling help reduce my *stress*?

The One Minute Sales Person responded, "First, let's realize that a little stress is, in fact, good for you because it sharpens your focus, and stimulates you.

"However, too much personal stress in your selling results in lower sales. Self-Managed Selling reduces your counterproductive stress in three ways:

"First, One Minute Goals help reduce anxiety, one of the greatest causes of stress. Anxiety is simply fear of the unknown.

"When you create your own goals and mentally see them as already accomplished in a peaceful, confident way, you lessen the unknown. You can see where you are going. It's like having a flashlight in the dark."

"Your point about seeing my goals clearly reminds me of when a friend of mine went to a car dealer in San Francisco. He was prepared to buy an expensive car that very morning. He stood in the showroom waiting—but he saw no one.

"Finally he stopped a lone salesman who was hurrying by him. 'Sorry,' the salesman said. 'I'm in a hurry now and I can't stop to talk to you.' Guess what he said the reason was for his hurry?"

The board chairman laughed and said, "Oh, no!"

"You guessed it," the man smiled. "The salesman said, 'I'm on my way to a sales meeting.'

"He had a chance to make a large sale with little effort, but he forgot what his goal was."

Both men shook their heads, knowing how easy it is for any of us to forget to do the obviously important things in selling.

"How do One Minute Praisings help?" asked the visitor.

"One Minute Praisings—catching yourself doing something right—reduce stress because they reduce fatigue. When you think well of yourself, it gives you a mental lift. It literally energizes you. The more often you honestly praise yourself, the less stress you feel.

"And One Minute Reprimands help you make more sales with less stress because they help you clear away your own obstructive behavior. There is nothing more exhausting than jumping over hurdles you continue to put in your own way. When you refuse to put up with such behavior, you rid yourself of a major source of stress. And, of course, when you reprimand the behavior but praise your better self, you reenergize yourself. You begin anew—refreshed.

"That is how the self-management part— Selling to Me—reduces stress. The other part— Selling to Others—reduces stress even more easily.

"When you Sell On Purpose," The One Minute Sales Person continued, "you don't swim upstream, fighting the power of reality. You realize that you do not control the other person and you never did. The only thing you have is influence.

"The more you let other people determine what is important to them and relate what you have to offer to how *they* want to feel—about what they have bought and about themselves—the more easily you will make sales.

"In fact: *You don't make the sale.* They *do*.

The visitor asked, "Is that why you put so little emphasis on closing?"

"Yes. Closing is needed most when you are trying to get people to do something they basically don't want to do. That is when some sales people start to press."

"I suppose," the man said, "that's how sales people got such a bad name."

"Of course," The One Minute Sales Person said. "But worse than that, it was unnecessarily hard on the sales people. They didn't need to be working as hard as they were. They simply needed to invest a few key minutes to find out what the other person wanted."

"That's like the best ads I've seen for personal computers," the man suggested. "They show a tired person who is not using a computer staying late at the office in order to get the work done. Then the ad shows a refreshed person leaving the office on time with all the work done and looking forward to an enjoyable event that evening. They didn't sell a product; they sold what the person really wanted."

The One Minute Sales Person asked, "What does that ad tell you about what people want?"

"It tells me that people are buying a personal computer for themselves not because they want to own a piece of equipment but because they want to have more time to relax and enjoy life more."

"Exactly. And how do you think that relates to why One Minute Selling works so well for sales people?"

The man thought for a moment and then replied, "I guess because each of the really important things we do in selling takes only a minute or so. If we'll just invest that important minute, we'll have more success and extra time to enjoy it.

"When we take a minute," he noted, "to practice what we know about the brilliant basics of selling, we make more sales, more quickly and with less stress.

"We're more refreshed and can enjoy the time we have left for ourselves."

"Now you've got it! One Minute Selling is not perfect and it doesn't solve all your selling problems all the time. But the point is it does work.

"You see," The One Minute Sales Person added, "you remember that effective ad because you have been thinking about what really works for a long time.

"You know what works. You've just let what you know get out of focus. If you remember to Sell On Purpose and to use the few brilliant basics regularly, you will experience the success you once had—and more! It is the natural way of selling."

The man stood up, shook hands, and thanked The One Minute Sales Person for his time and advice.

"I'm going to put what I know to good use." He smiled and added, "For the good of the buyer and for my own good."

The man left, feeling better already.

As the months passed, the man put what he had learned, or rather relearned about what he already knew, to *use*.

And the inevitable happened.

H E became a One Minute Sales Person.

It happened not just because he talked like one but because he had learned a better way to think and to believe—about selling and about himself.

And, most important, because over the years he frequently and regularly put what he had learned to good use. What he knew, he *did*!

While he varied what he actually did from time to time—adapting new ideas to new situations—he always relied on his solid foundation. He *Sold On Purpose*.

He was glad he'd learned that invaluable selling secret. It made everything else easier and more enjoyable—for everyone, especially for himself.

He shared this knowledge with others. He had even created a pocket-sized overall summary, a Game Plan for those who wanted to know his secret to success.

The man knew very well that the more he shared his success, the more success *he* would have.

A brief summary of

THE ONE MINUTE SALES PERSON'S

| I START |

with

MY PURPOSE

I help people get the feelings <u>they</u> want—soon!

SELLING TO OTHERS

Before the Sale

- First, I see other people getting the feelings THEY want. Then I see me getting what I want.
- I study the features and advantages of what I sell—thoroughly and often.
- I see the benefits of what I sell actually helping others get the feelings they want.

During the Sale

- I sell the way I and the other person like to buy. I invest time as a PERSON.
- I ask "have" questions and "want" questions.
- The difference is the problem.
- I listen and I repeat back what I have heard.
- I honestly relate my service, product, or idea only to what <u>the other person</u> wants to feel.
- The other person closes the sale when he sees he gets the maximum benefits with the minimum personal risk.

After the Sale

- I frequently follow up to make sure people are actually feeling good about owning what they bought from me.
- If there is a problem, I help them solve it—and thus strengthen our relationship.
- When they are feeling good about what they bought, I ask for <u>active</u> referrals.

SELELING TO ME

My One Minute Goals

- I write out my goals on a single piece of paper in 250 words or less, as though they were already real.
- I read/reread them in only one minute.
- Each time I reread my goals, I see them as already achieved.

Goals (Even Partly) Achieved

I WIN

My One Minute Praisings

- I frequently take a minute to give myself some "sales recognition."
- I catch myself doing something right! (or approximately right!)
- I laugh and enjoy telling myself what I did and how good I feel about it.
- I take the time to FEEL how good I feel about what I have done.
- I encourage myself to do this again.

Goals Not Achieved
(review goals)

I LOSE

My One Minute Reprimands

- I reprimand my behavior when it is unacceptable to me.
- I specifically tell what I did wrong.
- I let myself FEEL how I feel about what I did (or did not do).
- I remember that I am not what I do.
- I am a valuable human being and I deserve the best behavior from me.
- I get off my back and back on purpose.

MANY years later, the man looked back to when he first learned about One Minute Selling.

Since then, he had experienced both the personal and the financial success he was looking for. And had been recognized with a series of awards and promotions.

He was, in fact, like his original teacher.

He was especially glad that he had taken notes while he was learning how to sell from The Original One Minute Sales Person and his cooperative protégés.

His collection of notes allowed him to make copies of the text and share his knowledge of the selling secrets with new and veteran sales people more efficiently.

In his role as sales manager, it had saved him time.

And it let sales people read and reread the text at their own pace and as often as *they* found beneficial. He knew full well the very practical advantage of repetition in learning anything new.

After the sales people in his organization had read the text, he had made himself available for meetings, discussions, and workshops to help them put it to use.

It was most encouraging to see how quickly people thought up their own ways of Selling On Purpose—how they built on the value of trust and service and how they *did* the brilliant basics of selling.

But what was most encouraging was seeing how soon they improved their sales.

As more salesmen and saleswomen who worked with him became *self-managed* successes, The New One Minute Sales Person had more time to himself.

And as the people who reported to him became more prosperous, so did he. "The people who used to work for me made me look good as a manager," he thought, as he reflected on success.

Then he remembered what he had always known. "People don't work for anyone else. They work for *themselves*."

The One Minute Sales System was simply a way of people taking good care of themselves—from the person buying, to the person selling, to the person managing it all.

Perhaps what The New One Minute Sales Person enjoyed most was knowing that he didn't experience the daily emotional and physical stress other people subjected themselves to.

He was living and working On Purpose.

And he knew that many other people who worked with him enjoyed the same benefits.

His company had fewer costly personnel turnovers, less personal illness, and less absenteeism. The benefits were significant.

He felt capable of dealing with the present and well prepared for the future of sales.

T HE phone rang, bringing the man abruptly back into the present.

A young woman introduced herself over the telephone. She said she was a brand-new sales person. "I know I have a lot to learn," she admitted. "But I would like to learn from the best. Could I come and talk with you?"

The New One Minute Sales Person smiled.

It felt good to be in his position. He had certainly learned how to make more sales with less stress. He was, in fact, one of the most successful people in his field. And he was happy.

He had a good deal of time, now.

"Of course you can come and talk with me," he answered.

As soon as the young woman arrived, he began the conversation.

"I'm glad to share my selling secrets with you," the New One Minute Sales Person began. "I will make only one request of you."

"What is that?" the visitor asked.

"Simply," the sales person began, "that you . . ."

*

Share It With Others

*

Acknowledgments

We wish to give a praising to many of the people who helped make this a better book, including:

Peter Althouse, of P. K. Althouse Development for what he taught us about financial integrity.

Dr. Kenneth Blanchard, co-author of *The One Minute Manager* for his wisdom and support.

The Vice-Presidents of Marketing and Sales, National Sales Directors, and Sales People in many of the *Fortune* 500 companies and the nation's smaller businesses and general-interest organizations, for reading our manuscript and making suggestions.

William Gove for his continuing sales counsel.

Gerald Nelson, M.D., for originating The One Minute Scolding.

Abraham Maslow and Carl Rogers for what they and their writings taught us about what people want.

Margaret McBride for selling with integrity.

The Wilson Learning Corporation Sales Force, for the individual experiences and practical insights that they injected into this book and for helping provide better sales-training programs for business.

William Morrow and Company, our publishers, especially Pat Golbitz, and, of course, Morrow's marvelous sales people!

The buyers—literally thousands of buyers—for filling in our sales questionnaires over the last few years and speaking with us about how they liked to buy and what they really wanted in a sales person.

About the Authors

SPENCER JOHNSON, M.D., is one of the nation's leading lecturers, consultants, and authors. He helps people prosper by developing their own healthier communications, with themselves and with other people.

Dr. Johnson is the author of more than a dozen books on medicine, psychology, and business, including the best seller *The One Minute Manager.* Over seven million copies of his books are in use and his work has been translated into twenty-four languages.

He brings medical knowledge to public awareness by speaking to such groups as the American Bankers Association, AT&T, and IBM and by interviews with the national media.

His education includes a degree in psychology from the University of Southern California, an M.D. degree from the Royal College of Surgeons in Ireland, and medical clerkships at the Mayo Clinic and Harvard Medical School.

Dr. Johnson is chairman of Candle Communications Corporation, which develops communication ideas into audiotapes, videotapes, and microcomputer programs for business training.

He lives in La Jolla, California.

LARRY WILSON, educator, entrepreneur, and outstanding salesman, became the youngest-ever lifetime member of the Million Dollar Roundtable at age twenty-nine. Since the mid-sixties he has been a prominent speaker throughout the country on sales and personal growth, while bringing his sales-training company to preeminence in its field.

Wilson is currently directing, in alliance with the University of Minnesota, a learning consortium of universities and corporations and is building a conference center to house this consortium on his ranch outside Santa Fe, New Mexico. In recognition for his contributions to learning, he was named a Senior Fellow and faculty member of the University of Minnesota's College of Education in May 1984.

Larry Wilson presides as chairman of Wilson Learning, a firm that trains 185,000 men and women a year and has provided executive leadership for hundreds of companies worldwide. Wilson Learning, which now offers a One Minute Sales Person seminar, is one of the leading firms to promote audio and video training programs for business.

One Minute Sales Training

Our purpose is to help you get what you want, to help you make more sales with less stress. Reading a book can be very helpful in the pursuit of knowledge and we hope that this book has been useful to you in the area of personal selling.

We also realize that it is difficult sometimes to begin to *use* this knowledge as you go out into the world and try to sell your ideas, products, or services.

Therefore, in order to help you personally acquire the skills involved in One Minute Selling, we have created follow-up training programs for you to use—either individually or with a larger group.

These follow-up One Minute Sales training programs utilize time-efficient audiotapes, videotapes, microcomputer programs, and workbooks. If you wish further information about these programs you may contact:

Wilson Learning Corporation
6950 Washington Avenue South
Eden Prairie, Minnesota 55344
(612) 944-2880